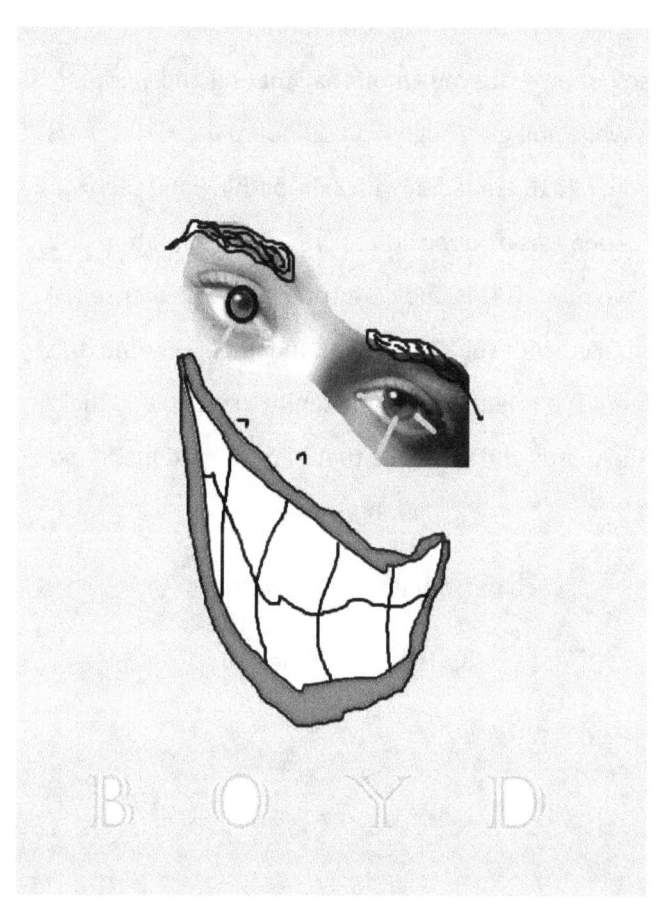

Welcome to an exhibition of me.

These poems trace my emotional, mental and spiritual states while going through high school to now. The years preceding 2016 are laden with self-loathing and teenage angst. Today, as a young adult, I've begun to mature and truly love myself. This book is a tribute to a former self. A person filled with self-doubt, fear and anger. For me, this document is a release. An opportunity to let go and make free the words and thoughts that had trapped me for so long.

Each person has their own story.

This is part of mine.

October 22, 2011

While Understood or Not

Once thought he was the only one who could understand

today, many steps passed;

realize that the strength didn't come from his hand

but from my notion of such facts, arose the strength

from within myself.

Evolution is much different in isolation,

thoughts need no emancipation,

for in my mind each thought is free

while understood or not

I am me.

<u>November 8, 2011</u>

More or Less

A fight between Myself

between what *was* known and everything else.

between what *is* and all the rest.

to determine what is or is not best.

to lay weight upon my breast ...

to have the possible indulgence in Stress?

to set out on *The* Impossible Quest

to seek more but end up with even less

<u>November 16, 2011</u>

Fragile Bird

I never realized how sensitive I was until I hurt myself

...

Until I went out of my way to do things that I know

are wrong

Until I am forced to pay the price,

to break myself ...

& become a fragile bird ...

June 25, 2012

Never to Accept

This world has taught us to judge, but *never to accept.*

Opinions, positions... that won't budge, advancement; for us, never towards the right step.

I feel at times I am the only one seeking light, dragging myself through life's sludge...

Each moment I die & I fester my might,

In my childhood dreams of life; I wish I could have slept.

January 29, 2013 at 11:54pm

The Void [Which is maintained]

That, which is mine, but I cannot regain.

This, which without, I can barely maintain.

Of which, I wish, to simply obtain.

But is kept by one who will not be named.

Save them, from the shame,

And withhold, for myself, the pain.

Although it pushes me towards insane,

I go on; living just the same.

May 6, 2013 at 12:58am

Times like These

It's moments like these that I have to beg

myself not to become entrenched in self loathing

it's times like these where I want to dress in only

black flowy clothing

I use the layers to cover up what I keep all from

knowing

Incessantly breaking; bend.

even if it's not showing.

Not sure whether I'm one broken thing

or broken things brought into one

a perfect picture?

but sideways I've been hung

childish ideologies unto them I should have clung

Alive today though, so I can still say I've won

June 29, 2013 at 12:53am

Attractive Mind

I like mind, I want to wrack it.

Unearth all the memories compact.

Creativity spewing through its eye;

It doth attract.

<u>April 9, 2014 at 10:08pm</u>

CYCLICAL HISTORY

Cyclical History

Fibonacci

Mystery

Repetitious

Delay

Create

Infinity

April 24, 2014 at 10:21pm

Like Humans

Loving her;
THAT doesn't make a lesbian.
It makes a human, and we like what we like.

...

Compassion created a human
But labels are man-made

...

Define the self by nothing
But experience in your shade

...

Man will try to tell you
"Your worth is worth your pay"

...

Designate you as numbers
And titles, such as "gay"

...

Do not be boxed or packaged
In prep to ship away

...

Maintain consciousness and liberty will stay

I love you

September 9, 2014 at 8:14pm

Don't

Don't get the attention

Not to mention

It is not needed.

Fleeted

Wanted is haunting

The present

Is whole in intention

And design

September 10, 2014 at 4:46pm

Sense of self

Establish & refine

Your sense of self

Then shit on it.

You are different

From no one else

September 21, 2014 at 7:05pm

The Sunset

Sensation of turbulence

Calmness of ease

Awe of Existence

MASTERPIECE

Exponential Taurus extension

(Perplexing in its peace)

Perfecting it's own power

For Eternity

October 9, 2014 at 7:23pm

Potential

Devastation ravages the soul who does not realize its

potential.

Potentially destroying the joy

Over self-proclaimed failures

Soul sailors; ship out

On the sea that is Mind

...

May the dawn awaken you

And allow you to find

The bliss in darkness

That amplifies the light

January 24, 2015 at 2:47pm

Its not for you to understand

Sometimes I want to cry when thinking about devotion.

Self debt that no one can repay.

The pain; Too great to quantify, to limit with such inferior words...

I believe we call it Life.

Friday, Sept. 1st, 2017

Twigs & Leaves
Season X
Chapbook Launch

Featuring:
Stephanie Azran, Naomi Boyd,
Russell Hartt, Noah Stevens
and more!

Time: 7:30
Location: Café T.W.I.G.'s,
85 rue ste. anne, ste. anne de bellevue
Wine, cheese & chapbooks!
$5.00 cover at the door (free for chapbook contributors)

<u>December 9th 2016</u>

Love, Lust & Crushes

Desires misdirected

neglected

withheld

Discomfort

pending sensation of Self

Reflection

Connection

Distorted perspectives

Innerstanding humans are their own

Respectives

September 20th 2016

Beaver Dams

Yearning long drawn out

'I can't hear you, the connection is breaking up!'

"DO YOU HEAR ME NOW?"

'I watched a video about beavers and it reminded me of you somehow...',

he had said once

'Such adorable creatures'

Funny how we make monstrosities out of our moods
And manifest our nightmares

Maybe we're just mirrors
& I'm searching for the right angle to take a selfie in
So that I can love myself

Peering into the reflection
A beaver healed me once
Upon reflection
A beaver helped me once
Interesting that I remind you of beavers
but you remind me of the dams they make
We are results of each other
A beaver
And the dam it has made

October 13th 2016

More than an archive

The struggle for survival is primal

I want to live a premium life

Grow like the trees and the plants…

More than just an archive,

Shifting in portrayal to give myself a chance

More than just survival

But a thriving romance

October 18th 2016

Equilibrium

The universe seeks to achieve equilibrium

Such are the rules of thermodynamics

I guess that's why you were taken from us...

The balance must remain

I stand still here, as you lay to rest

The time between our next meetings lessens

Here; Senescence

As I stand

Living here

Dying here

Awaiting Equilibrium

July 13th 2017 at 9:41AM

Cutting Ties

grow apart,

it hurts

expectations,

assumptions unlearned

make room for new things

Acknowledgements

Thank you to those people of my past and present

who were subjects of my writing.

My higher-power, who has allowed me to live and

feel a wide variety of emotions.

My mother for being the instrument through which

the noise of my life was born.

My first boyfriend who would leave me and catalyst a

streamline of experiences which without I would not

be here today.

And finally my first girlfriend, which is the subject of

an entire book to come soon.

www.ingramcontent.com/pod-product-compliance
Lightning Source LLC
Chambersburg PA
CBHW050039230526
45470CB00003B/1352